HAND ILLUSTRATED POSTAL ENVELOPES

HAND ILLUSTRATED POSTAL ENVELOPES

David Swales

The Pentland Press
Edinburgh – Cambridge – Durham – USA

First published in 1996 by
The Pentland Press Ltd
1 Hutton Close,
South Church
Bishop Auckland
Durham

ISBN 1-85821-316-9

Typeset by Carnegie Publishing, 18 Maynard St, Preston
Printed and bound at the University Press, Cambridge

To Meg

Contents

PART ONE

PREFACE

For me, the study of this subject has been a fascinating and rewarding experience. In particular, the practice of illustrating my own envelopes has given me much interest and pleasure. It all started several years ago when I read a review of nineteenth century pictorial envelopes in a copy of the English *Country Life* magazine, which is known for its well presented coverage of a wonderfully eclectic range of subjects. The article was written by Huon Mallalieu and, in the tradition for which he is famous, this polished commentator outlined and detailed this subject with well researched facts and interesting information. I could see immediately the potential that this charming and intimate art form would have if revived with modern ideas and techniques. I eagerly set to work to illustrate my own envelopes, but was hampered by a lack of suitable materials, and an even greater lack of artistic knowledge and skill; but as I persisted, the techniques developed and the results began to show noticeable improvements.

Since my searches for information on this subject have revealed only one book—which deals with nineteenth century pictorial envelopes, including some which were hand illustrated—and a total absence of material dealing with contemporary examples, I decided my ideas on the subject should be aired.

It will be seen that I have featured in Part Two quite a number of my own works. I argued that to make this subject interesting, a wide variety of examples had to be shown, ranging from those of the late nineteenth century to the present day, in order to give the reader a rounded picture of this minor art form. I therefore took it upon myself to design and produce a series of envelopes which would effectively present a range of some appropriate contemporary ideas. The alternative of locating enough suitable examples in private collections and postal museums would have been too time consuming, and many of the ideas I wanted to feature would not have been found anywhere, since they relate to aspects of life and attitudes of the second half of the twentieth century—basically, of my own lifetime. My readers must therefore understand this aspect of my presentation, and not look for artistic merit in the examples of my own work; the main purpose for their inclusion is to generate an awareness of the potential of this subject, and to provide a basis for instruction, ideas and techniques.

I have researched this subject in art houses, libraries and museums in Britain, Australia and France, and have found many interesting and beautiful examples, mainly originating from the 'Belle Epoque' era, *circa* 1900. Some of these I have featured in this book; to my mind they are representative of the best from this era—having the best artwork and the most imaginative ideas and techniques, even though, compared to the modern examples, they generally lack some of the technical complications and enhancements.

It is obvious that although there are many excellent nineteenth century hand illustrated envelopes extant, people interested in this subject, living a hundred years from now, will not have anything new to discuss or discover unless someone like myself is to initiate a resurgence of interest in it. I have therefore planned this book largely as a didactic discourse on the practice of illustrating envelopes in the hope that the specialised knowledge that I have gained in recent years can help others to enjoy producing their own envelopes and, thereby, give pleasure to their friends. I commend to my readers the challenge of illustrating their own envelopes—even if the quality of the artwork of the first attempts may not seem satisfactory, at least the ideas and overall presentation are sure to have a great impact on the people who receive them. An illustration can carry a very intimate message, one that usually doesn't require excellent artwork for it to achieve its purpose.

It is assumed in the following text that my readers have, like myself, only a superficial knowledge of philately and postal processes. More knowledgeable readers must therefore tolerate my amateurish but hopefully adequate remarks dealing with these matters.

As the title 'hand illustrated postal envelope' is quite a mouthful, I have given some consideration to coining a name for this postal item, but have so far not come across one which is suitable. The initial letters H I P E produce a valid word, but one which I find unattractive for this purpose. Throughout this book, for want of a better solution, I have used the abbreviated capitals 'IE', to differentiate it from the more general name of 'Pictorial' envelope.

The philatelic world is full of helpful, professional people, and it has been my pleasure to have met and corresponded with many of them in the past few years. Those to whom I owe particular thanks are David Boyd, Director of Phillips, London; Dr David Beech, Head of Philatelic Collections, The British Library; Mme. Auger and the staff of the Musée de la Poste, Paris; Ritchie and Gerald Bodily, London; Charless Hahn, Illinois; and Dr Chris Jarvis, Cornwall.

I am also very grateful to The Hon. Mrs Roberts and staff of the Royal Library, Windsor Castle, for information and research assistance.

1

GENERAL DESCRIPTION OF
HAND ILLUSTRATED ENVELOPES

Hand illustrated postal envelopes (abbreviated to IEs in this book) are those postal envelopes which have been decorated on the address/postage stamp face individually by hand, using any of the graphic techniques available to the artist. Such techniques usually involve the use of pen, pencil, or brush type artwork, but can also involve screen-printing or stencilling in conjunction with hand-colouring, hand-marbling, and similar combined procedures. As such, hand illustrated envelopes are individual works of art of a genre which is little known, the current practice of which must be one of the least common of all the minor graphic art forms.

Postage stamps have an important sociological role in bringing important issues and historically interesting subjects to the attention of the general public. Postmarks associated with stamps, which include a message or slogan, have a similar role. Illustrated envelopes, because they can carry so much descriptive material, interesting detail and subtle messages, can be very important social documents, and are therefore highly regarded as collector's items.

Any study of IEs will automatically refer to other closely related postal art forms, in particular the Picture Postcard and the Pictorial Envelope. Both of these postal items are usually found to have been printed, mostly using chromolithography and similar techniques, in large quantities. It has been estimated that in the year 1905, seven billion postcards were sent world-wide. It is also interesting to note, as Leopold Weiner observed, that, in regard to the physical dimensions of the postcard (or envelope for that matter), its size is the optimum for our eyes when viewing an image. When it is held in the hand, our eyes take in the whole picture at once.

Some of the *fin de siècle* artists who produced illustrations for postcards and posters are also likely to have produced small numbers of IEs, either for their own use or on commission. Very little can now be found out about this work; however, it is my estimate that largely because of the time involved in producing worthwhile IEs, the private rather than the public exposure of the work, and the possibility of damage or loss in the postal system, that the total output by recognised artists during this period could hardly have exceeded two thousand. These would be highly prized collector's items. Many more IEs of variable quality were produced by amateurs, some with a gift for this type of illustration, but the majority of these are less likely to have survived the last hundred years.

Because the great majority of artistic Picture Postcards of the 1890s were reproductions or adaptations of popular drawings, posters and paintings of that period—artwork originally produced for other reasons—it has been stated that there is little justification for regarding them as an art form in their own right. I suggest that in the case of IEs there is not the same stigma; in fact there are a number of factors which combine to make IEs a very unique genre.

Grouped with the Postcard and Pictorial Envelope are also the First Day Covers, Maximum Cards and Aerograms, all of which have been produced only in relatively recent years. All of these postal items usually incorporate a picture together with a stamp, printed in colour on one side. The picture usually takes up most of the left hand side of the envelope, leaving a blank space on the right hand side for the address to be written in. In addition to these items which are produced by the postal departments of various countries, there are the 'advertising' and 'propaganda' envelopes produced by private companies and corporations. Large numbers of these were produced in the last decades of the nineteenth century, and they are still being produced today by companies who feel their products or company services are appropriately marketed in this way. None of these cards or envelopes can be put in the same category or genre as IEs for obvious reasons, although the thematic linking of the picture and stamp subjects in Maximum Cards and First Day Covers is one feature of a good IE.

In comparing the fundamental differences between an IE and a Picture Postcard, we note that the postcard has one side devoted to the picture, and one for the name and address, message and postage stamp, while the IE must include the name and address and postage stamp all on the picture side. The reverse side of the IE of course need only have the sender's name and address. The picture side of the IE must therefore be planned carefully so that all the written information does not detract from the overall appearance of the illustration. This can require a good deal of ingenuity, depending on how serious one is about the illustration. On the other hand, if the illustration is confined to (say) the left hand side of the envelope, leaving the right hand side for the address and postage stamp, then the procedure is straightforward. This type of IE generally lacks interest, however, it being similar in layout to most First Day Covers, and it is not until we integrate the address and postage stamp into the design that we fully realise the uniqueness and character of this genre. Simply to paint a picture on an envelope, then to stick on any stamp and write the address in a convenient location has limited value as a meaningful communication, when compared to the unique, subtle, personalised versions that are now possible, with the help of a wide choice of beautiful stamps on a large range of subjects. The basic options available for the illustration of an IE relate somewhat to the artist's ability, although simple, amateurish pictures which carry a clever message or idea are very worthwhile.

In general, we usually see the following types of illustration:

(a)   The picture is restricted to the left hand side of the envelope and the right hand side is used for the postage stamp and address;

(b)   The picture covers the whole envelope, with postage stamp and address placed in convenient locations;

(c)   The picture is designed to incorporate the postage stamp and address;

(d)   As for (c), but with picture and postage stamp subjects thematically linked, perhaps also with other enhancements.

The possibilities listed in (a) to (d) above give an indication of the range of options available to the artist, without further mention of how aspects such as personalisation, for the recipient, can be incorporated, or how the monetary value of the finished envelope can be increased. These matters will be covered in detail later.

Regarding the quality of IEs, I see the main features of a good IE to be:

1.   The illustration contains a significant amount of original artwork of a high standard;

2.   The illustration displays a degree of design ingenuity to incorporate the necessary descriptive information and stamps, within the constraints imposed by envelope size, layout and function;

3.   The illustration contains a degree of personalisation (relating to the recipient) in the subject and/or the style of the artwork.

It should also be remembered that an envelope with a postage stamp is a collector's item. With an attractive or well designed illustration its value to collectors is greatly increased.

The aim of achieving a worthwhile combination of good artwork and an interesting design, resulting in an attractive and valuable collector's item, is the challenge of those who practise their skills in this area.

2

Origin and Development
of Illustrated Envelopes

Although machine-printed, mass-produced Pictorial Envelopes cannot be considered to form a prime part of the subject matter of this book, I propose to discuss this interesting area of postal stationery because there is no doubt that some early examples are entirely pertinent to the development of the IEs which were common in the late nineteenth and early twentieth centuries.

Cheap postage was introduced in Great Britain just over 150 years ago. The Mulready envelope was selected as a prime postal item by the British government from a number of proposals put forward. Its selection was also approved by Queen Victoria. The introduction of this envelope initiated an extraordinary, if predictable, series of events. It was produced by the thousands in 1840–41, and featured an impressed design (basically an arrangement of small engravings) and carried a postal value of one penny, or of two pence. The famous 'Penny Black' adhesive stamp was often stuck onto the envelope to enable the letter to be posted further afield. The envelope takes its name from the designer, William Mulready, RA (1786–1863), who was a noted artist of the time.

A copy of the Mulready design is shown here as illustration No. 1. It features the figure of Britannia, standing on a pedestal, with the British lion at her feet, the outstretched arms of the figure depicting the act of despatching winged messengers to all points of the globe. The top and sides of the design show miniature scenes of people in far off lands receiving or reading letters. The overall subject was evidently considered to be eminently suitable as an emblematic design, showing the benefits of the cheap postage introduced by Great Britain. The artistic design was '. . . deliberately chosen, with a view to elevating the public taste . . .' (!) The red Maltese Cross shown in this example was applied as a hand stamp by the post office to cancel the envelope.

On the days following the first public issue of the Mulready envelope, *The Times* newspaper featured letters from irate and disgusted citizens, ridiculing the design. No doubt some of this vitriolic attack originated from artists and engravers who were unsuccessful in having their own proposals adopted. One person wrote: '. . . Its trumpery appearance shows that it is a complete piece of Whig jobbery . . .'; and another: '. . . we never beheld anything more ludicrous than the figures or allegorical device by which it is marked . . .'

No. 1   A copy of a typical Mulready envelope.

No. 2   A copy of one of the famous Mulready caricatures by H. K. Browne.

No. 3   A copy of a Mulready envelope, coloured in using coloured pencils.

No. 4   The Mulready caricature by H. K. Browne, coloured in with Texta colour pens.

In a very short time, caricatures and imitations of the Mulready envelope began to appear. Some of these were designed by artists such as John Leech, Richard Doyle, and H. K. Browne, who were to become well known in their field. These caricature envelopes were printed by the thousands and are these days collector's items. A copy of one such caricature, by Browne, shown here as No. 2, would rank as one of the most popular at the time.

Some of these printed Mulreadys and caricatures were coloured in by hand, or were added to by those having some command of artistic skills and a more elaborate message to convey. Two of my own hand coloured Mulready copies are shown here as No. 3 and No. 4. Adding familiar names to the figures in the design (politicians, or even Queen Victoria for example) was a common practice, as were humorous comments or features. Even Mulready himself received one which had tails drawn on all the animals and people!

It is at this point that we perceive the beginnings of what has now to be regarded as a very fascinating graphic art form: hand-illustrating a postal envelope.

Once cheap postage was established, thousands of individual designs and inscriptions were printed on, impressed or embossed on envelopes for use as commercial advertising, or for propaganda and social statements. On viewing examples of this sort of printed stationery today, we are struck by many curious and amusing instances of social manners and customs, by the engraver's skill, and in general by the great variety of themes covered by this medium.

Military servicemen of the second half of the nineteenth century were particularly prolific in producing IEs. Their subjects related mainly to life and experiences in the

No. 5   An example of a typical hand drawn envelope done, with a touch of humour, by a World War Two serviceman. I can't read his signature.

armed forces, particularly the military, their letters frequently being posted from distant lands to their loved ones at home. The magazine *The Regiment*, which was published in England in the 1890s, promoted the use of IEs in the army. It ran regular competitions and published a number of articles on this subject, indicating the degree of interest shared by its readers. This is not surprising when we realise that one of the main leisure pastimes of military men when away from home is talking about and writing to their loved ones. For many amateur artists, the long hours of boredom must at times have been turned to good use as they practised their art on the envelopes which enclosed the letters they sent home.

The First World War was also responsible for generating a further output from servicemen, and after a general lapse in activity, World War Two had a similar effect. An example of a typical Australian soldier's IE from the 1940s is shown here as No. 5.

Since the 1940s, interest in IEs has almost died out. Relatively few articles have been published since then and a very sporadic output has been evident from amateur and professional artists alike.

Some of the most notable nineteenth century artists who have produced IEs are Hugh Rose, Arthur Ellis, Francis Herring, George H. Edwards, and Arthur Fredericks. I have featured the works of some of these artists in Part Two of this book to give the reader an idea of the style and characteristics of the better IEs of a hundred years ago. The envelopes produced by the watercolourist George H. Edwards in particular stand out as examples of very high achievement, from both a design and an artistic standpoint.

In regard to design complexity, it is obvious that few of the IEs produced before, say, 1930, could display an interesting illustration which was supported by a thematically linked stamp, since most stamps issued prior to that time featured only the Monarch's head, or a very limited range of nationalistic features. Artists of today can choose from an immense range of stamp subjects. Furthermore, artists of the nineteenth century generally did not have to contend with lengthy addresses and postal area codes, air mail stickers and the like, which clutter the illustrations of modern envelopes. The most basic facts were evidently satisfactory in the nineteenth century. In 1843, for example, we see the following:

Mr James Ray Jun.
Aberdeen

In 1854:

Dr Dick
Dundee

In 1860:

Miss Payne
High Street, Lewes

More shall be said about the problems and requirements of modern addressing later.

3

Uses of Hand Illustrated Envelopes

It is generally agreed that to receive a personal letter from a friend is a pleasurable event, provided of course that the letter does not contain bad news. In any case, it is usually a more forceful, more meaningful, method of communication than its main alternative, the telephone, whether for transmitting good or bad news. The power of the written word, the realisation that the writer has taken the trouble to compose a series of sentences containing information and comments solely for the recipient, goes to make the communication by mail a significant one, one the recipient acknowledges consciously or unconsciously—shown by the way personal letters are opened, usually with a feeling of excitement and anticipation.

The first reaction of one who has just received a letter is usually to glance at the handwriting for a clue to who the sender might be. Then perhaps the letter is turned over to check if the name of the sender is written on the back. If however the person is expecting good or bad news, for example a reply to a job application or examination results, these niceties are usually dispensed with in the haste of ripping at the edges of the envelope to open it as quickly as possible. Some people, on the other hand, prefer to put their letters aside until they are composed or settled enough to open them in a careful, deliberate manner.

What is the difference in receiving an illustrated envelope?

Quite simply, the IE enhances the excitement of receiving a personal letter. Once a person sees his or her name featured pictorially on an envelope, the attention is arrested immediately, and the person then focuses on the involvement of their name in the picture, and the meaning of such a communication, before opening it. The reaction of the recipient will depend somewhat on the type of IE and the content of the illustration or decoration, but invariably the person will feel a subtle sense of importance, mixed with pleasure (perhaps accompanied with laughter or exclamations of surprise), or just plain contentment that such a unique 'gift' has been received.

A good IE will often include in the illustration a personal message to the recipient, such as a reference to an occasion shared by sender and recipient, a reminder for a date, or just a humorous viewpoint of a personal characteristic. It will display, by means of the artwork, clever or subtle ideas, and it is these ideas contained in the design that give the IE its real character, its particular individuality.

Because of these features, an IE can be an extremely offensive instrument if it is illustrated with rude, provocative or sarcastic features in the picture. The effect it could have on the recipient in this case may be considerable, and it is certainly a fact that IEs have been used in this way as far back as the Mulready caricatures. There have been instances where the illustrations and messages on envelopes have been regarded to be so offensive by the postal authorities that they have declined to carry such mail. I am of the opinion that IEs should only be used for giving pleasure to the recipient, with open or concealed messages being well considered and executed by the artist. Such messages are fraught with the danger that they will be misread, resulting in a subsequent lengthy explanation of intent on the part of the sender.

To be specific, the main purposes of IEs are:

(a) To use a hand illustration to enhance the value of the envelope as a philatelic item;
(b) To provide an opportunity for people to enhance personal messages;
(c) To promote serious art, as applied to small-scale works;
(d) To promote interesting postal communications.

In the long term, when the reasons for the illustration—the message and the personalisation—are forgotten, it will be the value of the postage stamp and postmark, enhanced by the illustration, which determines the value of the IE.

4

Types of Hand Illustrated Envelopes

Broadly speaking, hand illustrated envelopes can be separated into two distinct groups. The first group comprises those which have been printed and have subsequently been hand coloured or added to, and the second group are those which have been illustrated by hand, starting with a blank envelope.

The first group includes all those which were originally intended to be complete, as Pictorial, Advertising or Propaganda Envelopes. Examples are:

(a) Pictorial Envelopes such as those on sale at post offices as Maximum Cards, First Day Covers and the like. These are mainly multi-coloured prints, and have been professionally designed in great detail. They are therefore not likely to be improved upon as works of art by the addition of further sketching or colouring. Around the turn of the century (*circa* 1900), a number of Pictorial Envelopes were produced for general sale to the public, in the same way as Picture Postcards are. An example of a First Day Cover is shown here as No. 6.

(b) Advertising Envelopes were used widely for all manner of services and merchandise, including foodstuffs, farm implements, fashion accessories, and theatrical shows, to name but a few. These were mainly mono-colour line drawings, decorations or sketches which included the advertisement or message as part of the design. Some were printed on special papers, or had embossed features, or were complete reproductions in colour of a company logo or trademark. Many firms today still use this relatively inexpensive means of advertising. Two examples, are shown here as No. 7 and No. 8.

(c) The Mulready envelope also falls into this general group. It was produced in large numbers in 1840–41, and lent itself to many degrees of caricature, alteration and imitation.

Envelopes in the second group are those which truly justify the title 'Hand-Illustrated', and will therefore be treated in greater detail.

There are a number of readily discernible levels of artistic achievement or difficulty associated with the design and production of envelopes in this group, so for the purpose of discussion and identification, I have broken the group up into five distinct categories, defining them as follows:

No. 6   A first day cover by Australia Post.

1. Artistic embellishment of the lettering or writing of the address; fine calligraphic work. The addition of minor pictorial sketches, located in the blank spaces around the address.
2. Loosely designed with decoration of a minor nature, e.g. floral border, bunch of flowers. With pattern, decoration or illustration separate (frequently on the left hand side) from the formal address block (right hand side).
3. Full illustration having blank spaces or plain coloured areas used for writing in the address, and for the stamp location.
4. Fully designed, with illustration subject and stamp subject thematically linked, and with elements of the illustration being specifically designed as appropriate spaces in which to write in the address and to locate the stamp.
5. As for Category 4, but also including one or a number of further enhancements which make it a more interesting, or a more valuable, postal item.

A list of some of these enhancements is as follows:

- The envelope is hand made, for example using coloured, textured or other special paper.
- There is a 'hidden' meaning or message contained in the illustration, intended for the recipient.
- The recipient's name has some connection with the illustration or postage stamp subject.
- A high value postage stamp is used.
- A set or series of envelopes is produced.

No. 7   Typical commercial (printed) envelope.

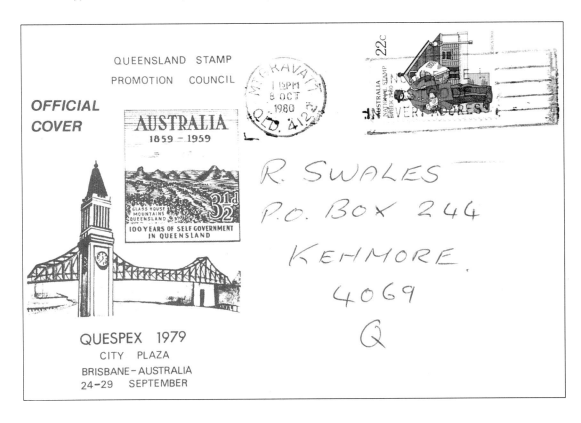

No. 8   Typical commercial (printed) envelope.

- The recipient is a distinguished person.
- Embossing or other special techniques are used in the illustration.
- Both sides of the envelope are illustrated.
- The envelope is signed and dated by the artist.
- Matching notepaper is used inside the envelope.

Out of some two hundred of the most interesting IEs taken from the period 1870 to 1910, I estimate that in broad terms, around 30 per cent would be Category 1 or 2 and 70 per cent would be Category 3, 4 or 5, but most of the Category 4 and 5 envelopes were understandably lacking the 'thematically linked stamp' condition owing to limitations of stamp subject during that period.

As many of the enhancements of the Category 5 envelopes are not readily apparent from photographs or even detailed descriptions, a true value judgement is not always possible. My general aim is to produce Category 5 envelopes, where some sort of message is conveyed to the recipient by means of the illustration, and where other enhancements are also included.

To produce a Category 1 or 2 envelope is for most people quite an easy task compared to producing a fully illustrated Category 4 or 5 type. The effort and time involved normally increases in proportion to the category number. As with other forms of human endeavour, however, if more work is put in, more satisfaction results. I find that the ideas are the main driving force in the effort I put in—if the ideas are good, then I am not content with a simple illustration.

5

Design Ideas and Sources

For those of my readers who might like to illustrate their own envelopes, I will now describe how I view the inspirational and thought processes which initiate and consolidate ideas for the production of an IE.

As is the case in all fields of art, inspiration is one of the principal formative ingredients in the production of a successful piece. In the case of subjects appropriate to IEs, ideas can originate from almost any source. It is obvious that to produce a Category 2 envelope, a fair degree of skill may be required for the artwork, but usually only a small amount of capability or flair is needed to handle the design task; complex ideas are not involved. It is quite a different matter to produce an IE of Category 4. In this case, a great deal of thought and design refinement is usually required in order to do justice to the task.

The overall value of the IE benefits from a serious attempt to find a subject with a high degree of interest, particularly for the recipient. Valuable inspiration can be triggered by witnessing an event which relates to the interests of the recipient. Alternatively, a session of brainstorming and quick sketching can often produce results. I have found myself sitting for hours doodling, developing an idea this way and that, without managing to hit on a suitable combination of elements which really satisfies. Then, all of a sudden, something clicks and it all falls into place. It helps to have a germ of a good idea in the first place as this can give you the confidence to persist with it until a good solution is found. The solution to the design can be very much like solving a crossword puzzle—deciding on one or two vital elements can mean that the rest falls easily into place. Leaving the illustration in an unfinished state, then returning to it a few days later, can also be very beneficial. Quite often, when reviewing an unfinished work, I have an immediate rush of further ideas for design options or refinement, and at this stage many changes to existing details can often be incorporated if required.

There seems to me to be little justification in outlining in any more detail the way I go about conceiving a design; every person has his or her own way of thinking these things through to completion, preferences for subject matter and so on. One general policy I adhere to, however, is that of originality in the creation of the images I put on the envelope. I personally disdain the idea of copying, and get a great deal of satisfaction from devising my own characters, postures, forms and arrangements. In some cases, because of the subject of the illustration, for example No. 48 and No. 82, accurate copying must be carried out in order for the illustration to achieve its purpose.

Without doubt, one of the principal components involved in the design task relates to language—the use of a vital group of words which communicates a message: the recipient's name and address. We see messages and notices everywhere—in our cities, our streets, houses, schools and work-places. The sporting equipment we use, the cars we drive, even the clothes we wear often have fashion labels, and a variety of slogans and place names. This 'commercialisation' aspect is only one feature which was missing in the world of nineteenth century artists. Our parks, rivers and beach resorts are likewise signposted, titled, advertised and illuminated with messages and signs.

An illustration itself can also provide a message without accompanying words, in the same way that a cartoon can be complete without any caption. Pictograms, which depict objects in a simplified way, and ideograms, which express ideas, are all part of modern day communication. For instance, consider the unalphabetic world of applied science, with its use of signs on remote controls for television sets and car dashboards.

Returning to the illustration of an envelope, one of the objects of our design task is to find or devise suitable locations or objects within the illustration on which to 'hang' our signs—the name, address and postcode. The solution can take the form of one location for all this information, or there can be a number of locations, one for each part or word. As mentioned above, the abundance and variety of signs found in our communities gives us good reason to include in our illustrations a selection of objects such as signposts, hoardings, posters, labels and notes, titles and direction boards, to name but a few. Consider also the example provided by some clandestine operators who use any accessible wall or large exposed vertical surface on which to paint graffiti messages. This is a liberal extension of the traditional advertising board or hoarding that we see next to our roadways.

Illuminated night signs can be as varied as a fertile imagination can conceive them, with brilliant moving, changing or alternating pictures. A fireworks display can be shown to explode a colourful message across the sky. Water skiers can be made to carve out a name in the wash of their skis. A teacher can write a message on the black (or white) board. Smoke signals from a camp fire can be yet another fanciful example. The number of these ideas, whether technically feasible, aesthetic, whimsical or far-fetched, is enormous.

There are many examples of artwork or design which are seen together with words or a short message. Posters, book and record covers, cigarette packets, food wrappers and labels, commercial advertisements, business cards and restaurant menus are some examples. Much can be learnt about the ways that these messages are used, and how they can be adapted for use with IEs.

As an alternative, the design plan for an IE can commence with the choice of a postage stamp, and then to design an envelope around it. I have found that a browse through a stamp catalogue can identify a number of stamps of suitable value obtainable from a stamp dealer which can be worked on to develop ideas for an illustration. No. 52 is an example which came from this approach. The extension of the picture around the stamp presented itself as an attractive solution, with the name and address integrated into the picture through the device of sand formations. A number of other options for inserting the address could have been used, but the idea of children writing in the sand seemed to be the most suitable one for the recipient I had in mind.

For a Category 4 or 5 IE, the character or interests of the intended recipient is normally the central issue in the decision-making process of what the subject of the illustration will be. Perhaps that person is celebrating a birthday, has just participated in a major sporting event, has a great ambition, has recently attended a wedding, or maybe has shared in some intimate experience with you, the artist. In particular, relationships and experiences shared between lovers provide many opportunities for 'secret' messages to be conveyed in IE illustrations.

Subject matter is mostly taken from aspects of everyday life, from folklore, customs, fashion, fantasy, poetry, religion and sport, to name but a few. The subject and details need not be of great general importance or interest, but if it relates to the recipient, then it has merit, and if rendered successfully it will be appreciated.

6

SUITABLE ART TYPES AND STYLES

Unquestionably, any type of art at all can be employed in illustrating an envelope, be it realist, impressionist, modernist or caricature. Just so long as it is a type that is suitable for the subject and the appreciation of the recipient, it should be successful, provided that the materials used are appropriate.

Some artists feel their style is suitable only for one medium, e.g. oils, and would prefer not to use anything else. This could create a problem with IEs, for instance in the case of oil paints, because the papers used for envelopes are not really suitable for this medium. I could also imagine that thick daubs of acrylics, as used in some modern abstract styles, may cause problems in some postal sorting and handling processes. Obviously, glued-on pieces of material and similar types of artwork would also be unsatisfactory for the same reasons.

I have observed that the genre of IE art more often leads the artist into the realm of realist or caricature/comic art types than any other. A survey of hundreds of examples reveals that the illustrations are either traditionally realist or are of a humorous, whimsical or sometimes satirical nature: in other words, very suitable for caricature.

Because most of the IEs we see today were produced in the 'belle epoque' era, *circa* 1900, there is no evidence of modern art types; they are almost completely missing from known records. This unfortunately is related to the decline in activity in the IE art form during the present century. I imagine however that artists of the modern schools would find interesting applications of their styles if they were to approach the illustration of envelopes with an open mind.

A further point to consider is the size of the envelope. Normal sizes are not large canvases, and can be totally unsatisfactory for some artists whose styles cannot be restricted to such small dimensions. It must be remembered that the envelope is intended to be held in the hand, not viewed from a distance of a few metres. There is the possibility that large envelopes can be made; however, in the postal handling processes these may suffer damage such as creasing and folding.

7

APPROPRIATE MATERIALS, METHODS AND TECHNIQUES

As mentioned above, some techniques and materials should by choice not be used when illustrating envelopes. The main restrictions relate to postal handling processes, which, in the modern world, make use of highly sophisticated automatic equipment, and therefore have certain practical restrictions. Other problems relate to the material of the envelope itself—normally paper—and the suitability of the illustrating medium.

One of the most important considerations is the choice of paint or medium. Basically, all commercially available mediums available today would be non-toxic and light-fast, but for our purposes, charcoal, chalks and pastels can be liable to smudging damage, and perhaps be irreparably damaged if soaked by rain, or if soiled, for example in a dirty letterbox. Even water-colours, which have been a popular choice of IE illustrators over the years, are susceptible to damage by water. IEs done with 'washable' colours such as acrylics are capable of withstanding a careful light sponging if surface dirt has marked the illustration. I have tried using inks, watercolours, acrylics and gouaches, oils, coloured pencils, texta pens and even vinyl house paints, and find that acrylics (often diluted with water) and pigmented inks are the most satisfactory from an overall point of view. A great many of the early IE illustrators used only black ink, possibly because they were worried about the water-damage aspect of watercolours.

The techniques for producing multiple copies, such as screen printing, stencilling, and linocut or woodblock printing are suitable provided waterproof inks and paints are used. If this can't be done then it may be possible to use a protective sealing spray on the finished work. My IE No. 58 is an example where I used acrylic paint to screen print the green stems, leaves and lower band. The flowers were then painted in by hand. The object of this particular illustration was to paint the roses similar to the one shown on the postage stamp. Using this procedure, each envelope printed can be different if each flower, or pair of flowers, and buds are given a different shape and colour. An alternative to screen printing many copies of the first colour is to obtain colour photocopies from the original, but only if the quality and weight of the copy paper is suitable for the subsequent work intended.

A further suggestion is to screen print the same base or background features onto a

23

number of envelopes, and then to print different second, third or fourth colours on each envelope to make each one individual—with no hand painting. This is obviously quite a lot of work and expense in terms of screen making, and would only seem to be warranted if hundreds of envelopes were to be made. This approach unfortunately decreases the value of the IEs produced because the subject chosen for the illustration would not be individual or personalised to any one recipient.

Hand marbling is another technique which, in the hands of an expert, can produce interesting and attractive patterns. Although each piece would be different, once again, however, the value of the envelope suffers from a lack of personalisation relating to the recipient and, furthermore, there is no opportunity to elevate its status above Category 3. A hand marbled envelope is shown as No. 23.

The method I use is straightforward. Assuming that a Category 4 or 5 illustration is intended, I start by drawing an outline of the subject in pencil, often followed by inking in some lines and details, followed by painting. Detailing with pen and ink is often the final step, together with writing the address, which is sometimes a full-scale calligraphic effort. I find that inking of some lines is necessary on normal sized envelopes to achieve details which are sufficiently effective. The first stage of pencil work must be planned to allow adequate areas for inserting the name and address, and also the optimum place for the postage stamp or stamps (and perhaps an air mail sticker). This presupposes that the stamp size and shape are known, as is the address, otherwise a generous allowance must be made.

Aspects such as size of envelope will be dealt with in some detail later, but the point can be made here that the large sizes are more likely to be damaged in the handling process, not the least likely culprit being an irascible postman who finds that the envelope doesn't fit conveniently through the slot in the recipient's letterbox.

The material of the envelope must of course be compatible with the illustrating medium used. Postal envelopes are made from paper which is normally not heavier than 100 grams per square metre. It is possible to use water-colours and acrylics on this lightweight paper if care is taken, and if a small amount of distortion or crinkling can be tolerated. I prefer not to be so restricted, and cut my own envelopes out of 160 g. s. m. Canson Mi-Teintes paper, which is readily procurable in large sheets, in white and many other shades, from art supply shops in my area. Even with this weight of paper, a wash of paint laid over a large area can result in some minor distortions of the paper. I have also used oil paints on this 160 g. s. m. paper with some success, but prefer not to be bothered by the lengthy drying times involved.

The procedure I adopt in preparing an envelope is first to cut out the shape of the envelope from a large sheet of paper, then to attach this directly to the drawing board without folding it. Once the illustration is complete, I fold the paper into the envelope shape and glue down the side and bottom flaps, leaving the top flap free until the letter is inserted, then it is lightly stuck down with glue, or with adhesive tape.

The brushes I use are a mixture of round and flat shapes. The one I use the most with acrylics would be a 2mm tapered round shape, of sable hair. The pens include a set with calligraphic nibs, and a Rotring pen with various point sizes, mainly used for ruling lines and for some printing. I also use conventional ink nibs for sketching, and I often need the finest point I can get.

A basic assortment of drawing instruments—rulers, set squares, compasses, shape templates, French curves, etc.—is essential, as is a selection of paint palettes, mixing dishes, clean up cloths, adhesive tape and glue. Particularly important is a good sized work table or drawing board with a comfortable chair or stool, and with good natural light if possible. I also make use of a large magnifier/light mounted on an articulated arm, to assist in completing fine details.

It is necessary to remember that when it comes to addressing the envelope, some inks are dye based, and will smear if the envelope gets wet. For normal correspondence this is not a very important point, but with IEs all necessary precautions should be taken to safeguard the artwork.

8

Design Details, Hints and Information

Because IEs must be regarded as special letters, owing to the artwork involved in the illustrations, a number of the considerations outlined below, which would be tiresomely elementary if applied to normal letters, will be treated as matters of importance.

The overall layout of the envelope, oriented either horizontally (normal) or vertically for reading the address, should allow for the postage stamp to be located in the top right hand quadrant, preferably close to the corner. The address, whether in one block or separated into a number of elements, should be located somewhere in the centre or the lower part of the picture, with the postal code preferably in the bottom right hand quadrant. There is no doubt that if these features were to be completely jumbled, the sorting mechanisms and staff of the post office would somehow work out the correct address, at the cost perhaps of some minor irritation. In my view, nothing is gained by deliberately planning an illustration to make life difficult for postal workers and their automatic machines, although I am guilty of one breach of this code myself. One of my illustrations featured the inside of a restaurant, the central view being out of a large window on which was printed in large letters the address of the restaurant (the address of the recipient). The problem here was that the words were all back to front, because for the purpose of the restaurant the address was to be read from the outside. As the lettering was large, the address was very easy to read, even though it was back to front, but some postal worker decided there was a need to write the address the correct way around at the side of the illustration, thus making a mess of the picture. I learnt my lesson from that experience, although I think the illustration idea was a good one all the same.

After a letter is posted, a cancelling postmark is applied over the postage stamp as one of the first steps in the handling process. This ink impression states the time and date, and the place where the postmark was applied—the nearest mail centre to where the letter was posted. Other features or messages usually also form part of the postmark. As this impression should always contact at least a small part of the postage stamp, much of it could be struck over parts of the illustration, obliterating some of it. As the date details should always be readable, it is therefore wise to arrange that the parts of the illustration in this area are not important and of pale colours. It is possible in Australian post offices to ask the postal worker behind the counter to apply the postmark by hand-stamping in the location of your choice.

No. 9   A special pictorial postmark used by Australia Post.

Special postmarks, because of their wording and design, can constitute a worthwhile enhancement to the value of the envelope if the subject is thematically suitable. The same goes for the cancelling stamps applied by automatic handling machines. Some examples of these are:

'Pollution Common Cause For Concern'
'Child Safety Is No Accident'
'Include Postcode In Every Address'
'Correct Addressing Saves Us Guessing'

This last one would have been very appropriate had it been stamped onto my 'restaurant' envelope mentioned above! An example of a special pictorial postmark is shown here as No. 9.

Regarding overall layout, a choice should be made at the outset as to whether the illustration will be 'free form', or whether it will be enclosed within a border line. If a border line is used, it must be decided whether it should be thick, thin, wavy, coloured or otherwise. Often, the detail of the border can be a final step in the process, especially if it is only going to be a plain straight line, square corner type. It can be quite surprising to see how the final touch of adding even a plain border can alter the appearance of a design. Some decorated borders can be integrated into the illustration as a major feature of the design, in which case full attention to this is imperative from the beginning.

It should be understood that if a letter is wrongly addressed, or needs to be re-addressed by the post office or a person who wrongly receives it, the illustration is more than likely going to suffer some damage. As the design of many IEs doesn't allow for extra information to be written in on the illustration, the new address or alterations will possibly be hand written somewhere on the illustration, and the incorrect address will be crossed out. This would be a great pity if the original address was a calligraphic masterpiece, not to mention the disappointment suffered by the recipient in seeing a nice picture disfigured.

Regarding wrongly addressed letters, or just badly addressed letters, I think the post offices do a wonderful job to decipher bad writing and incorrect spelling, and to handle so many odd and sometimes ridiculous items. I take my hat off to staff of the British Royal Mail service who successfully delivered a postcard simply addressed to 'Edna, Nick and Family', and signed 'from Bren and Anita'!

Calligraphy can form a significant part of an IE, since the name and address of the recipient must be included, and the overall design of the illustration could dictate that a specific style of lettering should be used to enhance its appearance. Calligraphy as an art form is now widely recognised, and it is therefore possible to produce an interesting IE solely of calligraphic images. On a less specialised plane, however, it is still necessary to have a working knowledge of common types of lettering—Copperplate, Art Deco, Italic, Gothic, or maybe Carolingian Miniscule!

It is a pity to see good illustrations with poor calligraphic efforts, or with a style of writing or lettering which is inappropriate for the illustration subject. Above all, the address must be readable without difficulty, which implies that the size of the lettering must be large enough for normally sighted people, and the arrangement of lines should be made to read from top to bottom. I suggest that depending on the illustration details, the inclusion of the recipient's surname is not always necessary, although it is always preferable. Hyphenated surnames and some lengthy (Welsh?) place names can also present difficulties in terms of space requirements within the illustration. Preliminary planning can be essential.

The practice of embossing names and other details on envelopes can be seen as an attractive enhancement. It is appropriate for many styles of lettering, and can also be used for highlights or even full decorative borders. I have used gold and silver embossings, and find the technique simple and quick to do, even on the thicker grades of paper.

I invariably work on hand made envelopes. These usually measure 220mm x 110mm, which is the DL standard size. I cut these out of a sheet 750mm x 550mm, from which I get six. With this size envelope, I have found that there is a limit to the size and quality of detail that can be achieved, even working with a magnifying glass. In some cases I have found the finest nib point to be inadequate. When I have completed the illustration, I sign and date it on the back flap, and number it.

It is now possible to use computers to produce graphic mono or multicolour images, as instructed by the programmer and operator. This can be another way of producing an IE, especially for people who are not 'pen and brush' artists. Patterns or geometric designs and lettering in particular would be straightforward to do, and the 'trial and error' facility of colouring in and shading various areas should ensure a good result. If no colour printing unit is attached to the computer, a picture could be copied from the screen by hand, or coloured in from a black ink output.

Regarding security within the mail service, it must be acknowledged that an IE is a fairly 'high profile' postal item compared to a normal private or business letter, and it can be specially scrutinised by post office employees and procedures if the address details or stamp location is irregular. Furthermore, if singled out for detailed scrutiny, post office employees could take quite an interest in it—for instance if it contains a humorous cartoon picture, or if it is signed by some well known artist. I hasten to add that I have never lost an IE, but I have had two torn open whilst in transit in the mail system, and a few have taken many days longer to arrive than they should have done. I can imagine that the fear of having IEs 'souvenired' by someone in the postal system is a deterrent to some well known artists who might otherwise become involved with this genre.

The value of postage required for a particular letter depends on the physical dimensions and weight of the letter, and its destination address. Different categories, such as Air Mail, also apply. When designing an IE, I try to use postage stamps which have a value greater than that which is required; in some cases it could be many times greater. This is not only a gesture to the postal department for the possible extra effort needed at times to handle these letters, it is also in the interests of producing a valuable postal item.

The monetary value of an IE can be difficult to determine. Aspects such as the intrinsic value of the stamps used (and their condition), the eminence of the artist and the value of the illustration as a work of art (or just as a social statement) are some of the main factors. The postmark details, the name and address, and consideration of any other enhancements can also be important. There are obviously many valuable IEs in existence, bound in bundles in musty rooms, in the possession of families who regard them as important records of their family histories, which will never be valued or offered for sale. In other situations, the value of personal letters can be extremely high because of an emotional attachment between the people involved. It is always advisable to keep the letter and envelope together for these reasons. Value also attaches in the case where an envelope is one of a set or series, or simply if a collector just falls in love with it. In short, if an IE is regarded as a work of art, the same value principles apply as for most other art forms. If it is regarded as a simple postal item, then normal philatelic values would be applied.

PART
TWO

PREFACE

The selection of envelopes featured in the following pages commences with some beautiful examples which originated in the last years of the nineteenth century and early years of the twentieth century. Following these are some later twentieth century envelopes from my own collection. The remainder were produced by myself in recent years and I thank the recipients of these IEs for allowing me to show them in this book. In all cases the name of the artist is given if it is someone other than myself.

My envelopes are numbered in chronological order of the date they were executed or date stamped, but they have been renumbered consecutively in the following pages to provide a clean format. The numbers are helpful for identification and referencing purposes. It will be noticed that many of my envelopes were sent to relatives, in particular to my daughter Celia during a period when her address changed at regular intervals. At least if her name gets boring to my readers, her addresses add some variety to the illustrations.

Before photographing some of my recent envelopes, I had to mask out elements of the true addresses by over-laying fictitious ones, as requested by the recipients, so that they retain their privacy. This is understandable and is a small price to pay for being allowed to present this material. The envelopes themselves have not been defaced in this process, only the photographs of them show the changes. I retain authentic records of all original works featured.

Beneath each example, I have provided descriptive information regarding the subject of the illustration, postage stamp, address, etc., perhaps with some anecdotal or background notes associated with the recipient or the reason for the illustration. In some cases details are also given of the materials and mediums used.

Finally, I present a brief list of the artists or illustrators known to me. It was not my aim to make this aspect a prime feature of this book and it is possible that some serious omissions have been made. It is hoped however that this brief survey will assist and possibly encourage others to enter this field to work towards producing a comprehensive catalogue of these works.

Regarding a bibliography of works on this subject, the book by Ritchie Bodily, Chris Jarvis and Charless Hahn, *British Pictorial Envelopes of the 19th Century* (The Collectors Club of Chicago, 1984) is the only one that I know of which features pictures of IEs. The

E. B. Evans book *A Description of the Mulready Envelope, and of Various Imitations and Caricatures of Its Design, with an account of other illustrated envelopes of 1840 and following years* (Gibbons, London, 1970) is also interesting. Apart from these, the Sale Catalogues of the International Philatelic Auctioneers: Phillips, Harmers, Christies, Stanley Gibbons, etc. give a great deal of information and pictures, mainly of nineteenth century and early twentieth century envelopes. There have also been articles featured in various stamp magazines and other periodicals.

No. 10   This is an envelope by the watercolourist Hugh Rose, who served on the staff of The Prince of Wales. It appears that many of his envelopes were sent to members of the Royal family; these at recent auctions fetching bids up to £4000. This particular envelope is kept in the Royal Collection at Windsor Castle. The envelope size is approximately 460 x 300mm. The Royal Collection © Her Majesty The Queen.

No. 11   The Prince of Wales at an Exhibition.

No. 12   Herald holding up a scroll.

Nos. 11 & 12   These two envelopes were done by Sir Arthur Ellis, who was Equerry to The Prince of Wales from 1866. They are typical examples of his watercolour illustrations, and are kept in the Royal Collection, Windsor Castle. In this case only the fronts of the envelopes are kept, as they are mounted in a scrap book. The Royal Collection © Her Majesty The Queen.

No. 13

No. 14

No. 15

No. 16

Nos. 13, 14, 15, 16 These are typical examples of French IEs done in watercolours by Facteur Pioche. These are part of a collection of his envelopes kept in the Musée de la Poste, Paris. All were done in the period 1907–1910.

No. 17

No. 18

No. 19

Nos. 17, 18 & 19   These are examples of propaganda illustrations done in 1947 by C. H. Hollis.

No. 20   An example of a simple hand painted decoration. Artist Unknown.

No. 21   An envelope by Sonia Stratton who is well known for her hand painted versions of British First Day Covers, which she has exhibited at Stampex in London. This envelope measures 240 x 165mm.

No. 22   An envelope by Ann Willers, sent to her daughter in Cairns. The butterflies are a species indigenous to the Cairns region; all the more reason for Ruth to like the envelope.

No. 23   My daughter has a compulsive desire to experiment with all sorts of artistic techniques. Hand marbling is one that has fascinated her and, being in the position of not having an instructor, she has experienced some degree of frustration in grappling with the materials and skills necessary to achieve what can only be called modest results! I was really very pleased to receive it.

No. 24   This envelope was one of my first attempts. It was done as a kind of copy of a well known painting by R. G. Rivers called 'Under the Jacaranda'. The copying aspect was intended to be good enough to be recognisable to the original, but it also had to be adapted for the purpose of including the address. The original painting is a favourite of my daughter, hence she is the recipient. A typical Category 3 envelope.

No. 25 One of my early illustrations. For the whalers of the nineteenth century, killing a whale was not an easy business, and the contest was arguably more in the whale's favour. I would judge from the illustration that on this occasion the harpooner is a little late in throwing his harpoon—I think the whale is safe!

No. 26 The reason for sending this envelope is obvious. The use of a postage stamp in a picture frame hanging on a wall is a common device which can be utilised in many instances.

No. 27   This picture takes me back to my boyhood, when my brother and I used to read adventure books like *Coral Island* and *Robinson Crusoe*. Whenever we had the opportunity we would see films of these stories, and we were always sketching and painting pictures with boats, tropical islands, warring natives and the like. Writing the address details in the sand is a suitable idea in this case.

No. 28   One of my early illustrations, using the subject of advertising which we commonly see at sporting venues. There are many postage stamps dealing with sport, and quite a few on cricket alone. A typical Category 4 envelope.

No. 29 Many boats these days have signwriting applied to their hulls, and most of it is of a much more elaborate and colourful style than that shown here. To do a good job of this lettering could take a lot of time especially as the area of paper is quite limited in size, and the perspective is difficult.

No. 30 The only real stamp here of course is the one on the right hand side. The Copperplate style of writing is fairly suitable, although it doesn't really match the style on the stamp.

No. 31   This envelope was originally purchased with a greeting card. The picture on the card showed a woman dressed in Victorian costume sitting on a grassy slope overlooking a vale, with distant buildings, etc. My idea was to paint a picture which matched and extended the card picture to the right, so that a more panoramic effect would be achieved if the card and envelope were placed side by side. I arranged a slight overlap of the envelope on top of the card, so we can just make out the back part of the woman's dress on the left of the envelope picture. Unfortunately, the matching card has been lost.

No. 32   The current popularity of roller blade skating is only meant to be of secondary interest here. The main ideas are the signpost (a popular device for IEs), and the 'vote' poster for the postage stamp.

No. 33   When my daughter rang to say she had just booked a ticket to come and visit me for a few days, the idea for this illustration came to mind, so I quickly painted it and sent it off to her. It is a good example of the use of a message which is only fully appreciated by the sender and the recipient.

No. 34   An excellent vehicle for the address location is the shop front window, which these days is usually full of messages and signs. As is shown here, irrelevant words can be modified by the interference of a vandal ('psychologist' crossed out and 'dreamer' inserted), to add interest, and perhaps insult, to the recipient. My daughter knows when I try to be humorous, and doesn't take offence.

No. 35   My intention here was to do a picture for my daughter of a happy childhood scene which had a lot of action in it.

No. 36   This gold medallion is another rather simple illustration which turned out to be quite effective.

No. 37   My daughter's favourite children's story is the fantasy tale *The Talking Parcel*, by Gerald Durrell. The illustration on the cover by Ann Meisel was adapted for the purpose of this envelope. The toadstool postage stamp is thematically linked to the illustration; although I also had the option of using a parrot stamp, I thought this was better.

No. 38   This simple sort of illustration is very suitable to send to a child (or in this case a cat lover). The kittens were added to provide a linkage to the stamps.

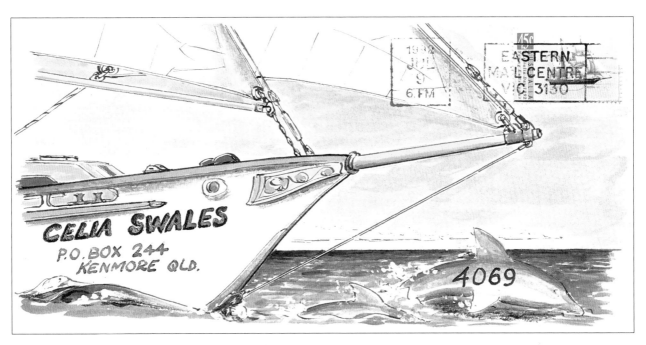

No. 39   This is the first of my illustrations done on 160 g. s. m. paper. The benefits compared to the 80–100 g. s. m. papers were immediately recognised, and I have been using this paper ever since. The choice of postage stamp for any sea scene is easy, since there are so many which feature boats, yachts and ships.

No. 40   Tom seems to have a lot of trouble with the cats in his area, so I thought this little picture might make him smile.

No. 41

No. 42

No. 43

No. 44

Nos. 41, 42, 43 & 44   This set of four sea scenes was painted with each of the stamp subjects in mind. They were to have been sent to my father, who passed away before I got around to sending them. This is why they are shown incomplete. My father was a keen yachtsman, and I can imagine the sort of conversation we would have had about the illustrations. His inquiring mind would surely have revealed some technical fault or improbability, but he would have appreciated them all the same.

No. 45   I sent this letter to the author Anthony Burgess only a few weeks before he died, so I imagine he may not have even seen it. The design was copied from the end papers of one of his books, and shows the sort of design that wealthy Elizabethans favoured for their pillow covers— embroidered on linen in silk and silver-gilt and silver thread.

No. 46   Fanciful, whimsical; an unusual illustration with a little humour thrown in. I have called this one 'The Monument to Famous People', so the postage stamp is quite appropriate, commemorating two Australian explorers.

No. 47   This is a very appropriate subject for our purposes—the signboard. I thought of increasing the interest by including details of the picture which was being covered—a very well known one, while conveniently not having to give the full details of the new picture.

No. 48   Here, I copied Michelangelo's great painting showing the creation of man—the part which was eminently suitable for the recipient in this instance.

No. 49

No. 50

Nos. 49 & 50   These simple illustrations are admired by the female members of my family. For each of these envelopes, I painted the enclosed notepaper with the same floral vine, which added to the impact of the communication.

No. 51   This picture was intended to be in the style of the Art Nouveau postcards of the 1890s, and the lettering was done to match. There was no suitable 'tennis' stamp available, so I settled for the floral one.

No. 52   'A Holiday at Mentone' (near Melbourne) was painted by Charles Conder in 1888, and is reproduced in this $5 stamp. Since the particular area of beach shown in this painting, and the pier, where now only a remembrance plaque sits, was where I often used to play and swim with my brother and sister as children, the painting is dear to our hearts. It is therefore a good stamp to feature on an envelope to my brother. In the 'extended' picture, the two boys could be taken to be me and my brother in the 1940s, superimposed on a typical 1880s beach scene.

No. 53 This rather enigmatic piece was conceived with a particular friend in mind who has a great diversity of interests. The dodecahedrons floating through space are intended to give the impression of a timeless environment which frees the brain of many conventional restrictions.

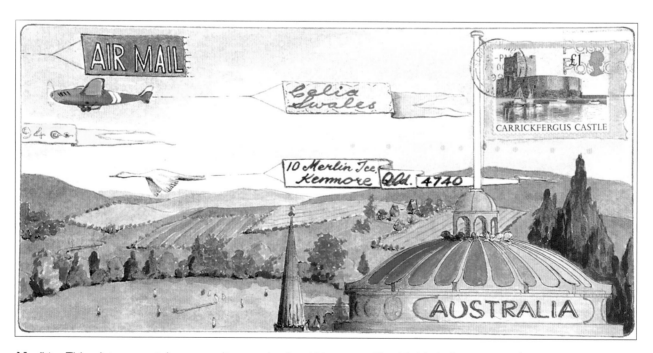

No. 54 This picture contains some 'tongue in cheek' humour. The bird is in fact not towing the small sign, as it might seem at first glance—a glimpse of the towrope for that sign can be seen on the far left of the picture, indicating that there is another plane involved which is out of the picture to the left.

No. 55   The liberty I took with this film title was intended to be a little dig at my daughter—the sort of thing she enjoys. Either postage stamp would have been sufficient to send this letter, but I preferred the arrangement shown.

No. 56   My own 'Australian' version of the Mulready envelope is shown here, in typically sober style characteristic of the original, rather than in the riotously funny or sarcastic styles of some of the nineteenth century caricatures. The postage stamps of the Forbes and Launceston post office buildings were selected partly because these buildings were both built in the latter part of the nineteenth century when the Mulreadys could still have been in use. For the sake of completeness, I add that my transposed picture elements show, on the left hand side, an aboriginal at his camp fire reading a letter, an Australian lyrebird, and a sheep station owner riding to his mail box to collect his mail. On the right hand side is a scene relating to the establishment of British sovereignty in Australia—raising the British flag.

No. 57   To copy pictures or patterns to a relatively small scale can sometimes take many hours of work. As the pictures used here are so familiar to most people, I thought a fairly accurate job was warranted to give a good effect. The Joker is of course my own version. The choice of stamp subject was basic to the design, as was the 'Q' for Queensland. A category 5 envelope.

No. 58   My sister has a successful business based on the screen printing and hand painting of colourful patterns onto ceramic tiles, which are used by home decorators as borders and features in bathrooms and kitchens. For this envelope, I used one of Ann's nylon screens—the 'Tudor Pattern', to print the green base lines and stems of the pattern with acrylic paint, then hand painted the two rose heads and buds as a copy of the postage stamp picture.

No. 59   This is another example where public signage is used to carry the address details of the recipient. This is also an example where the postal code can be included as a valid part of the illustration.

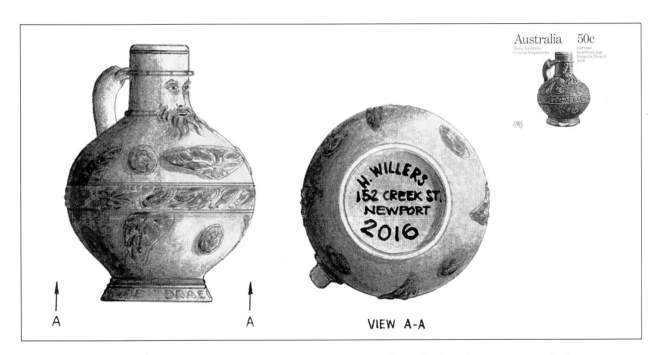

No. 60   On looking at the Beardman Jug stamp, I got to wondering whether there was a maker's name inscribed on the underside of it, as we see on most pottery and porcelain these days. This then gave me the idea for this illustration.

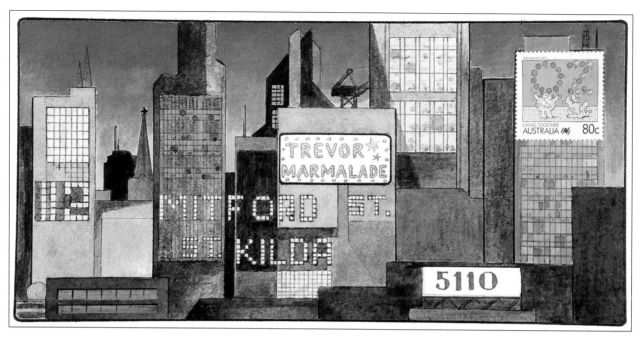

No. 61   This cityscape, titled 'The View From Jason's Penthouse' was done for my comedian nephew, who is a denizen of the throbbing night life of our big cities. To properly capture the idea of on and off lights in city buildings to form words can be quite a time consuming job, so I tried a few short cuts.

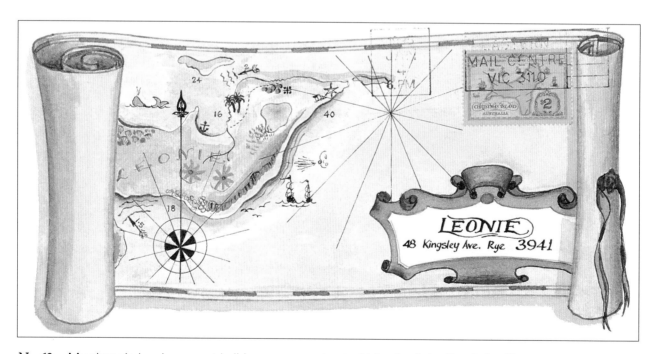

No. 62   My sister in law has spent holidays on many tropical islands of the South Pacific; however, she may not have been aware of this one named after her.

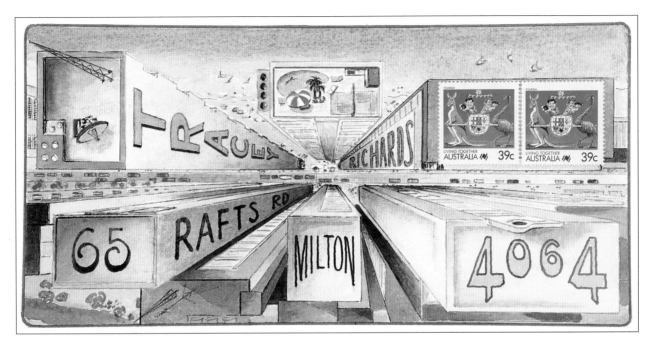

No. 63   The advertising signs, names and logos displayed on the sides and tops of buildings are a very suitable subject for IE illustrations. For this design I adopted an aerial view for maximum interest. As Queensland's Gold Coast is arguably the tourist capital of Australia, I thought the tourism stamps were a good choice.

No. 64   My daughter enjoys a little humour, so I sometimes send her an envelope of this nature. On the back of this one I added a quote of her saying: 'Oh my God, what has he done this time!'.

No. 65

No. 66

Nos. 65 & 66   These two envelopes represent my first attempts at producing Art Deco style patterns, which would hopefully appeal to both male and female friends alike. The dedication of two or more areas to stamp locations is straightforward in such a design, allowing the use of a pair, or even complete sets of stamps, if desired, on the one envelope. Although these designs are non-specific with respect to the personality or interests of the recipient, good examples must nonetheless be regarded as pleasing to look at.

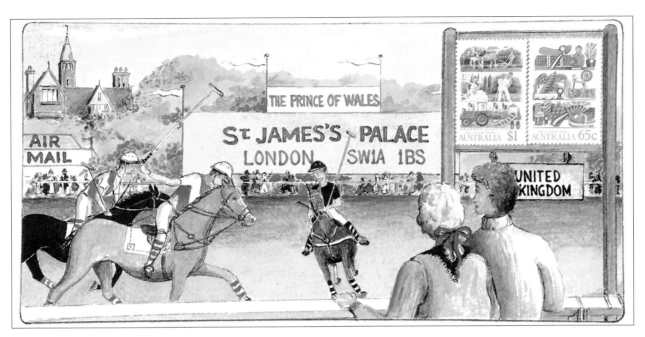

No. 67   Two of Prince Charles' loves are playing polo and painting, so I decided to paint him an IE of polo players. I would be naive to expect that he would have the time to devote to painting an IE in response for a person he does not know; my hope is simply that he got a little pleasure from my humble efforts. When I set to work on this illustration, I had never drawn or painted any animal seriously, so I studied pictures of horses, polo equipment and clothing, to give me a basic idea of what was required, then made up the design. None of the players in the illustration is intended to have a likeness to the Prince, nor are the 'colours' of the players meant to be authentic. Reproduced by gracious permission of The Prince of Wales.

No. 68   With only a small scale (postage stamp size) picture of Queen Victoria to work from, it's no wonder there's not a good likeness in my illustration. This envelope should really be sent to a person named Penelope Black, but as I don't know anyone of that name, I'll probably end up sending it to one of my philatelic friends.

No. 69   The subject of this illustration, and the device of using sail markings for the address, are not unknown in pictorial envelopes. A detailed knowledge of many aspects of the marine scene provides me with a facility of execution which I wish I had in other areas. Having a good knowledge of a subject means you can incorporate many authentic details, which add interest to the picture in a general way.

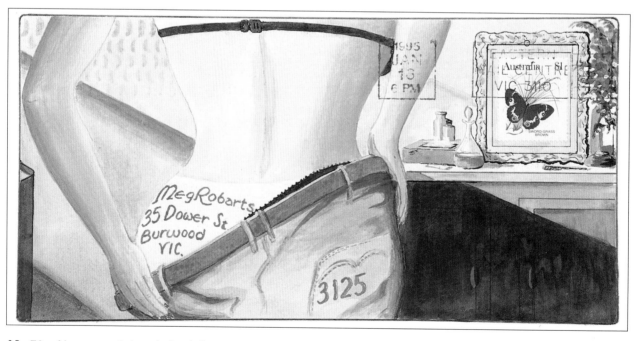

No. 70   Names and descriptive information are found in all sorts of places. A tattoo might be a good way of remembering your name if you happen to be forgetful, but also to tattoo your address may be a bit unwise!

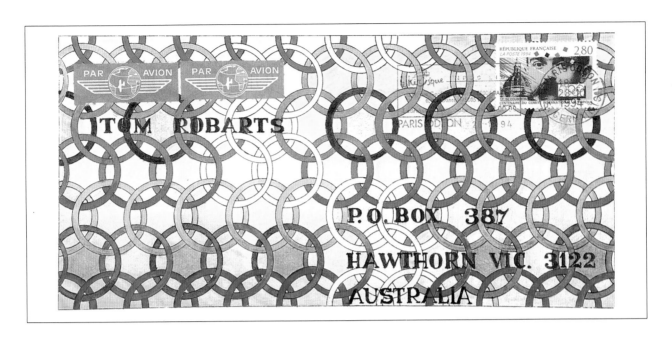

No. 71

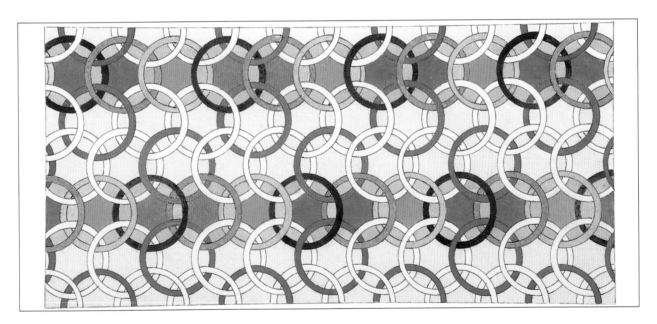

No. 72

Nos. 71 & 72   I found this fascinating chain mail detail (in use in the eleventh century) in the famous book of costumes by Auguste Racinet. I have since seen a piece in the British Museum which gives the impression it has been through a few battles! I see the basic element as two adjacent rings intersected (threaded) by one lower ring. To this can be added any number of rings, each arranged to pass through the two above it—a simple task for any medieval blacksmith! These two examples give some indication of the huge variety of colouring options available. I still haven't decided how best to stamp and address No. 72; perhaps the stamp should be a smallish one, and the address should be made to look as though it is written behind the mail. Before colouring this pattern, I did a few photocopies of the original so I could do some trial versions of colour arrangements. Here I used a combination of coloured pencils, watercolours and inks.

No. 73   I gave this illustration the caption 'Cat on a hot tin roof' to add a little humour. Ink sketching can give good effects, but I prefer the challenge of working in colour.

No. 74   The colourful designs now commonly used on hot air balloons make an ideal subject for an IE. In this respect, balloons are similar to yacht sails, where identification markings, numbers and messages can form part of the decoration.

No. 75 This was a rather quick and simple illustration, to convey a simple message. The basic idea of attaching an address note to some object has many applications. A typical Category 2 envelope.

No. 76 At this time, I was keen to try painting a variety of facial expressions. The strange thing is that (quite unintentionally) one of these singers bears a striking resemblance to a young woman I used to know!

No. 77   The idea of using gaily coloured fairies to adorn the letters of the recipient's name seemed appropriate in this instance. The style of lettering struck me as being of a suitably whimsical nature.

No. 78   This is a typical fanciful children's picture adapted to include appropriate spaces for the name and address.

No. 79 My cousin John is a sculptor, who would love to get his hands on a piece of marble like this. It might take him years to decide what to do with it, but in the meantime he would probably chisel his name on it. This envelope measures 220 x 155mm.

No. 80 I had initially intended doing a full mosaic picture, but found there is a lot of labour involved, so I settled for this simple one. The postage stamp is of 'Mimi Spirits Dancing'—I hope they have something to do with gardens and pathways!

No. 81 One of the disadvantages of an illustration having large blocks of heavy colour is that the postmark can be totally lost in it and be unreadable. In this case, when I come to send this envelope, I shall put the address on the horizontal red band, and ask the person in the post office to put a hand-stamped postmark on the red band also, so that it is readable.

No. 82 With apologies to Henri de Toulouse Lautrec, I copied the greater part of his picture 'Le Divan Japonais', and extended it to provide spaces for the address elements. To enhance this piece, I posted it from Paris.

No. 83 The birds here are all cut out from used postage stamps, and stuck onto the envelope. For someone having limited artistic skills, this idea could be exploited.

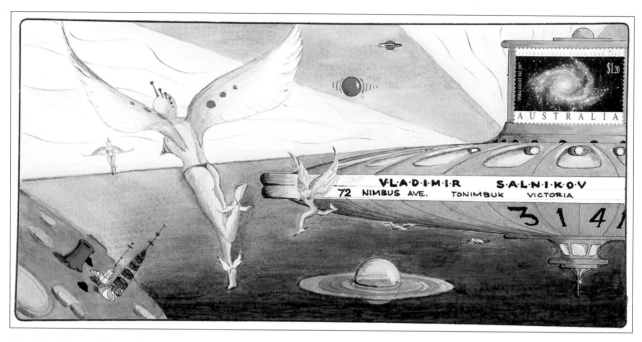

No. 84   The subject of an illustration does not need to be of a conventional nature. The meaning contained in this rather far fetched example (which I have captioned 'Winged aliens from space ship 3141') can only be guessed at. For a friend interested in *Star Wars* and Sci-Fi, such a picture could impress and intrigue.

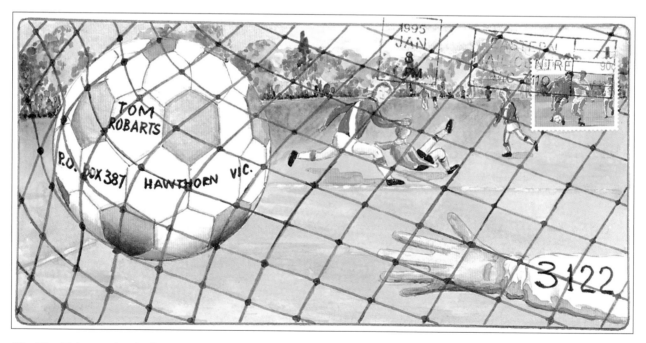

No. 85   This was basically an exercise in draughtsmanship—to show the ball and net in fairly accurate detail, together with some action figures in the background. As most people have a favourite sport, it is a good general subject to use for IEs, especially as there are so many sporting stamps available.

No. 86

No. 87

Nos. 86 & 87   The act of vandalism known as graffiti writing, on external walls of buildings, in public toilets and the like, can be most annoying to the owner of the wall. Many ancient drawings or writings scratched onto cave walls are now regarded as national treasures, as is the case of Australian aboriginal cave paintings. They were never regarded as defacing the surfaces they were drawn on. It was therefore particularly appropriate to use postage stamps of aboriginal cave pictures for one of these envelopes (No. 87).

No. 88 The timeless acanthus motif is used here as an example of a basic decoration. Combining to make the envelope a little more interesting is the attractive address label, and pretty stamp of an orchid flower.

No. 89

No. 90

No. 91

Nos. 89, 90 & 91   This group of Christmas illustrations provides a few examples of a large range of subjects available. No. 91 shows what can be done with simple colourful elements such as bells and ribbons, and some good lettering. Santa and his sleigh full of presents, No. 89, should appeal to children, while the trumpeting angel, No. 90, which I have captioned 'Move over bambini!', is a little more subtle.

No. 92

No. 93

Nos. 92 & 93   I painted these envelopes as a pair—the demure young woman with her fan, which perhaps she would be inclined to open out when in the presence of a young man, and the confident young man who openly displays his name on his folio.

No. 94   As my niece Lisa is a solicitor, this illustration is quite appropriate for her, as of course is the postage stamp. The little people holding the lettercards can be imagined to be the characters who have emerged from the books on the shelves.

No. 95   This simple but effective idea of showing the envelope as though it was being torn open gives this IE a bit of interest. The glimpse of the enclosed card was also made as interesting as possible.

No. 96   This cartoon is obviously based on the St. Trinian's school subject originated by that great artist and cartoonist Ronald Searle. I have given it the caption '. . . but Mr Fothergill, my girls are little angels'—with apologies to Mr Searle.

No. 97   Another of my favourite cartoonists is Thelwell. Many of his cartoons show rural English scenes, frequently incorporating the trials and tribulations of children learning the skills of horseriding. I have given this one the caption '. . . but it was the rabbit's fault!'—with apologies to Thelwell.

No. 98   With this envelope I made a 'toast' to my daughter's good luck in the future, as she embarked on a new phase of her life. The postage stamp, a Christmas issue, was quite suitable in this instance.

No. 99   The use of images and messages displayed on a computer screen offers a number of possibilities for IEs. I'm not sure what Magnetic Resonance Imaging is, or is used for, but the general idea of this illustration seems okay.

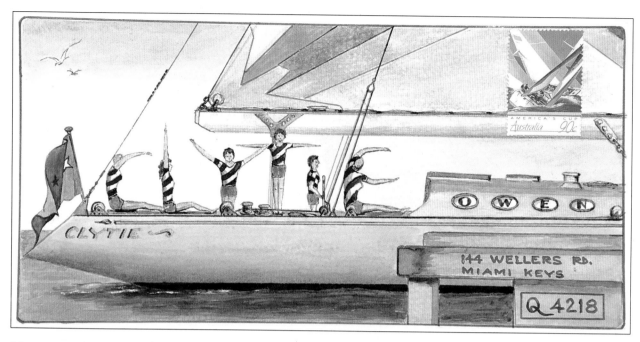

No. 100   My niece Clytie is very fond of sailing and, if I'm any judge, we will one day see her at the helm of her own large yacht. The idea of using human figures arranged in poses to represent letters of the alphabet has been employed by many artists. In this example, the concept of shipborne semaphore strengthens the basic idea.

No. 101   My interest in Antarctica was given a boost when my daughter gave me a book on this subject. This IE was simply a communication to her that the book was appreciated.

No. 102   The need for two of these skiing stamps to meet the postage rate was not a problem for this illustration, which, being quite simple, was quickly accomplished.

No. 103   Sailing ships have a wealth of fascinating detail for marine artists to put on paper. This illustration is typical of the type of scene sketched, usually in sepia tones, by the great marine artists such as Arthur Briscoe and George Gale in the early years of this century. I gave this illustration the caption: 'Fair weather and a landfall'.

No. 104   I don't know what my opera-singing niece thought of my elementary little composition—I suspect she might have had a good laugh at it. The postage stamp is well linked to the subject.

No. 105   This example makes full use of simple calligraphy to incorporate not only the postage stamp, but also the picture.

No. 106   Meg is a keen embroiderer, so I thought up this rather simple illustration with her in mind.

No. 107   Rodin's sculpture 'The Thinker' seemed the most appropriate subject to link up with this postage stamp, called 'Thinking of You'. It was also a good subject for Tom who is a great admirer of Rodin's work.

No. 108   The use of propaganda and also of 'outline' writing are not new to IEs. This envelope was made wider than normal so that a better idea of tree height could be shown. The envelope measures 220 x 155 mm.

DETAILS OF ARTISTS OR ILLUSTRATORS WHO ARE KNOWN TO HAVE PRODUCED ILLUSTRATED ENVELOPES

Many of the illustrators of IEs could be called accomplished artists. Comprehensive details of the *fin de siècle* illustrators are difficult to obtain, but it seems that not many of them were professional artists. The same can be said of twentieth century illustrators. In some respects this is not surprising, when we realise that for someone earning a living with pen and brush, there is no income resulting from the time spent in producing IEs for a friend or relative. Furthermore, the effort expended may not bring pleasure to the recipient if the letter were to be lost or damaged in transit. If professional artists take a negative attitude to this work it is understandable, but it is also an unfortunate loss to relatives and others who might otherwise have gained enjoyment from their work. I often wonder how the great modern caricature artists—Löbbecke, Petty, Nicholson, Searle and Giles to name a few—would handle this medium. With their levels of imagination and artistic skills some truly amazing works would be done.

We know of a few fine watercolourists who produced IEs. Many of the others who have signed their works can be regarded as accomplished or gifted amateurs, while many are the work of people having limited artistic skills but nonetheless with good ideas and a good reason to illustrate an envelope.

Basic details of the artists known to me are given below.

W. Adams
Twenty-two envelopes. 1916–19.

Hugh Benson
Corresponded with H. E. A. Platt. Various media. Two envelopes. 1898–1900.

A. Carson
Pen and ink. Three envelopes. 1869–95.

A. Geo. Chapp
French caricaturist and watercolourist. Pen and ink. Five envelopes. 1894.

Henry Culshaw
Ink and watercolour. Three envelopes. 1861–72.

Burgoyne Edwards
Relative of George H. Edwards. Ink and watercolour. Eleven envelopes sent from Montreal to various relatives in England. 1902–05.

George Henry Edwards (1859–1918)
Watercolourist. Exhibited at the Royal Academy and Royal Institute. Fourteen envelopes sent to

various relatives. Some envelopes sold in excess of £3,000 at recent auctions. 1885–1912.

Sir Arthur Ellis (1837–1907)
Equerry to the Prince of Wales. Watercolours. Eight envelopes addressed to the Prince of Wales and to other Royals. From 1867.

James Fahery
According to a Phillips catalogue of 1990, an IE by Fahery of the inside of Gwydyr Isa castle was sent in September 1822. This would make it the oldest IE known to me.

Fred Fegrum
Pen and ink. One envelope. 1887.

George N. Foote
Mixed media. Two envelopes. 1908.

Simon Fieldhouse
Ink and watercolour. Sixty-two envelopes. 1981–95.

Arthur Fredericks
Watercolour and ink. At least five envelopes. 1885–1911.

Kate Greenaway (1846–1901)
Professional artist, especially of children's book material. Watercolour. At least three envelopes.

Francis Herring (late 1850s to early 1930s)
Great-nephew of artist J. F. Herring (1795–1865). Pen and ink. Twenty-four envelopes. 1873–98.

G. Den Hartog
One envelope as a POW. 1901.

C. H. Hollis
Watercolour and ink. Four envelopes. 1947.

Colonel Hudson
Watercolour. One envelope. 1876.

A. Jimenez
Watercolour. One envelope.

Isaac Joubert
As a POW he did many envelopes for himself and friends.

S. W. Lawrence
Watercolour. Five envelopes. Late 1800s.

Karl Lewis
Did many IEs, usually of native scenes.

Reginald Linstead
Watercolour. One envelope. 1880.

C. Luteridge
Pen and ink. One envelope. 1886.

S. Malan
Watercolour. One envelope. 1901.

Harold Edwin Mosscrop
Pen and ink. At least seventeen envelopes. 1893–1903.

Bert Offord
At least four envelopes. 1924.

H. R. Palmer
Watercolour. One envelope. 1907.

Loftus Perkins
Pen and ink. Twenty-two envelopes, 1893–1902.

Facteur Pioche
French caricaturist and watercolourist. Watercolour. Eleven envelopes 1907–1910.

H. E. A. Platt
Corresponded with Hugh Benson. Mixed media. Two envelopes. 1889–99.

Collingridge Rivett
Watercolour and ink. Did many envelopes for himself and friends, some during World War 2.

Hugh Rose
Served on the staff of the Prince of Wales. Watercolour. Seventeen envelopes sent to the Prince of Wales and other Royals; also a number sent to Mrs King-Harman. Some envelopes sold in excess of £4,000 at recent auctions. 1896–1916.

Karl Sammuel
Scenery and costume designer. Sent a number of envelopes to relatives.

Kate Sherrin
Watercolour and ink. Four envelopes. Around 1887.

Sid Smith
Watercolour and ink. Eleven envelopes. Around 1920–30.

Harold Smith
Son of Sid Smith. Watercolour and ink. Three envelopes. 1923–7.

L. Lorraine Smith
Watercolour and ink. Three envelopes.

Sonia Stratton
Acrylics. Many hand-painted FDCs. From approx. 1980.

Celia Swales
Marbling oils. Two envelopes. 1994.

David Swales
Various media. In excess of 160 envelopes. 1990–95.

C. J. Tanner
Watercolour. One envelope. 1919.

H. M. Walker
Pen and ink. Four envelopes. 1909–11

Ann Willers
Acrylics and ink. One envelope. 1995.

Chas. A. Wilson
One envelope. 1902.